Talking to a Shaman

First published 2016 by
Aeon Books Ltd
118 Finchley Road
London NW3 5HT

Copyright © 2016 by Anthony Bogrjantseff

The right of Anthony Bogrjantseff to be identified as the author of this work has been asserted in accordance with §§ 77 and 78 of the Copyright Design and Patents Act 1988.

All rights reserved. No part of this publication may be reproduced, stored in a retrieval system, or transmitted, in any form or by any means, electronic, mechanical, photocopying, recording, or otherwise, without the prior written permission of the publisher.

Translation by Svetlana Shirley

Cover Image by Anthony Bogrjantseff
Illustrations by Svetlana Shirley
Design by Alexandra Thornton

British Library Cataloguing in Publication Data

A C.I.P. for this book is available from the British Library

ISBN-00: 978-1-9046587-1-9

www.aeonbooks.co.uk

Talking to a Shaman

Anthony Bogrjantseff

Aeon Books

Contents

Acknowledgements vii

Preface 1

   1 The first meeting with a Shaman 3

   2 The song of four elements 18

   3. A candle in the dark 28

   4 Stepping into the unknown 39

   5 The cart of life 48

About the author 55

A special thank you to Svetlana, who made publication of this book possible.

*In order not to fall down you need to
simply keep moving forward*

~A. Bogrjantseff

Preface

Somewhere deep inside each and every one of us lives our own wise man, a prophet or a shaman. He can be described in many different ways, but regardless of how we define him the meaning does not change. He is a higher inner being, a source of wisdom we all have, but barely ever touch.

Of great importance is the fact that this powerful and wise source of strength, this inner shaman, is available to all. He is capable of taking us unharmed to the very edge of the precipice, he can give us thousands of words of wise advice on any subject, and he can explain to us both the meaning of life and the essence of everything that surrounds us. Whether we are capable of taking in and accepting the wisdom offered to us is not relevant, but what is relevant is that this wise man can explain it all using words so simple they are understood by all, which is what makes him so priceless.

Some people recognise that they have the opportunity to tap into this bottomless pool of knowledge; they are aware of their inner 'shaman' and regularly use this endless source of guidance and acumen. However, even amongst those who have this awareness, there are people who cannot access their 'inner being', and cannot reach into this fountain of wisdom available to them.

Why are they not taking advantage of this free and readily available advice? I do not know. Perhaps, some people do not make the effort to open their mind and soul. Perhaps, they don't have enough patience to listen. Or perhaps, they simply cannot wait because they have no peace within themselves. Maybe, in some people, this wise man is hidden too deep inside their soul and their mind, and the wisdom is too difficult to uncover. Who knows? I most certainly do not.

Chapter One
The first meeting with a Shaman

My personal shaman, who lives in the depths of my soul, is called Wind of the North.

***

The footpath running through the musty grass was already touched by the ground frost giving it a mysterious blue tint. The trail was twisting around the roots of pine trees. The sky was clear, and the stars lit up the footpath, with the light sufficient enough for me to see the way, and where I was putting my feet. The walk was easy despite being a long one. I walked along the footpath and kept looking up at the night sky, replaying in my mind the short conversation I had had with the person who brought me here. He had not told me his name, or anything else for that matter. He had only given me directions.

"Where did you bring me? Where are we? I asked to see the shaman, but there is no shaman here!" I was indignant, thinking this was a waste of time.

"Why, what made you think the shaman would be waiting for you right here?" I could sense an irony in these words spoken by my guide, who had driven an old jeep to this seemingly godforsaken place. "Just keep going forward, the footpath will bring you to the shaman. Make sure that you do not miss your step, though."

After giving me a few more brief instructions, the driver got into his old battered vehicle and drove off. I had no choice but to follow his advice and continue my way on foot. Walking alone through the woods at night brought little comfort, and I was less than happy. Little did I know that the following minutes (or hours?) were going to change my life forever.

From my guide, I knew that the shaman I was about to meet was called Wind of the North. According to the driver, this shaman is one of the most powerful and wise in this area, and was respectfully dubbed as "Talking to the Spirits". He was said to be able to see beyond the human soul and heart, and beyond the understanding of any human being. This sounded scary and intimidating before I had even met him, but I wasn't going to give up.

"How can he call this summer?" I growled unhappily after I had slipped on an icy path several times. The footpath was damp and slippery, dry brown leaves had already fallen off the trees, and were plastered to the muddy foot trail. My shoes were sliding when I stood on those damp leaves, and I kept tripping over the tree roots sticking out of the ground. To keep my balance, I grabbed hold of the nearest branch of a fir tree. The tree needles stuck into my hand but I ignored this, because, as the branch bent under my arm's weight, the most unusual sight appeared in front of my eyes.

This picture was unforgettable. I saw a fire burning in the middle of the night forest, with its bright red flames aiming higher than the woods. The fire, the flames seemed alive, as if they were trying to escape from the constraints of a fireplace made from rough stones. These were laid down in a circle that was rather misshapen, and without any proper outline. It was difficult to say whether the person who had created this fireplace was unfamiliar with geometrical shapes, or was incompetent in setting up a fire. But, perhaps, it was quite the opposite – a wise man had designed this weird looking circle for a reason known only to him. The longer I looked at the blaze of the fire, the more I was inclined to believe this line of thought.

An old man sat by the fire. He was half hidden by the flames, and I understood he must have been the shaman I had come to see, my personal shaman, Wind of the North. He sat immersed in his own thoughts. Trying to be very quiet so as not to disturb his peace, I walked towards the fire and carefully perched my bum on the thick log nearby. The log was positioned on the side of the fire opposite to where the Shaman was seated and I reckoned it was the best place for me. Using this log as a bench, I sat at what seemed a safe distance from the flames and from the Shaman. I felt quite intimidated and wanted to have some sort of a barrier between him and myself, in case he would become angry with me. I was not sure why or how I could annoy him, because I came here to listen not to talk, to receive but not to give advice, to learn but not to teach. Nevertheless, I thought it better to be safe than sorry.

The Shaman sat very still with his eyes shut; he was seemingly oblivious to my arrival. After a short while, his lips trembled once, then again, and for a third time, and finally I could hear some kind of muttering. It was as quiet as a whisper and totally incomprehensible but I listened and watched attentively, in case there was a hidden meaning. How was I to know? Little by little, the Shaman started to gently sway his body in rhythm with his quiet murmur. He first began to rock his head from side to side and then his body started to shake gently, accelerating to a measured spin around in circles from the waist up. Suddenly, I realised the Shaman was not simply whispering, he was singing!

His extraordinary song was getting stronger and louder, his voice was gaining power and the song sounded more distinct, grew beautiful and melodic. The song seemed to be falling from the sky and onto the valley as a waterfall of sounds, resonating in the woods, spreading through the forest, uprooting the thick pine trees and cedars, which had been growing here from the beginning of time. My own life, in comparison to these trees and to the all-consuming power of this unearthly music, suddenly appeared as an insignificant and short episode in history.

The Shaman was powerful, indeed. Even though he had not said a word yet, this feeling could not escape me. Not only could he hold this great power over the forest and the fire burning in the middle of it, under his control, but he also was able to manage and direct it. The Shaman waved his hand and a tambourine suddenly appeared in his fingers, as if by magic – I had not noticed and could not understand where it came from, but could only hear its bells pulling me into a whirlpool of unfamiliar energy. The song now

Chapter One: The first meeting with a Shaman

sounded different, accompanied by the rhythmic beats of a tambourine and the gentle chiming of its bells.

I began feeling dizzy and could not vouch whether it was the tambourine bells or my own blood pulsating in my ears that contributed to the sense of total detachment from reality, a sense of total vacuum encircling my mind. My eyes felt tired and my eyelids heavy, but this magnetic song was still flowing, penetrating my every pore and taking over my consciousness.

At some point, I felt my mind drifting away and separating from my body, as if the Shaman and I had continued to sit as we were in our physical bodies but at the same time our spirits had moved out. Strangely, I was not frightened or even surprised by this; somehow, I must have expected something like it to happen. I sat with my eyes shut and my body swayed to the rhythm of the tambourine, synchronised with the moves of the Shaman. At the same time, in my spiritual self I opened my eyes and looked at the Shaman. The Shaman's body was also sitting with eyes closed and continued singing the same monotonous melody, while his spirit was positioned right in front of my own immaterial double. The fire was glowing between the two of us just the same, except the flames now seemed slightly translucent.

The Shaman lowered his head forward very slightly, and it seemed that he was looking at the fire through closed eyes, the flames still vigorously burning in their hearth.

"Our souls hide not only the knowledge of life but our fears, too. Remember that, young man," said the Shaman, addressing me.

The spirit of the Shaman was talking in the same manner

as his physical body was singing – unhurried, without disturbing the steady and measured rhythm of the song still echoing through the woods.

"The majority of your fears only exist in your own head. It is very common for a man to run from his fears, driven by the unconscious. When you find the courage to stop running and quietly examine your own fears, doubts and insecurities in the bright daylight of your consciousness, it will become apparent they are hollow and purely the product of your own thinking. You emphasise your fears, you imagine them being bigger and stronger than they really are.

Most people keep feeding their own fears by running from them, thereby allowing their worries to grow and expand, and to gain so much more strength that the problems completely overtake them and get embedded in their life. Instead of spending some time trying to understand and see their concerns for what they really are, to recognise them and to work on finding a solution; people put too much effort into running away from their problems. The problem may have been small but the longer you run from it the bigger it grows, if it is left unattended. There is no escape though, for while you run from the problems, they will keep following you. The time is irreplaceable, you cannot turn back a single second of your life. You could have dedicated some time to resolve the matter troubling you while it was small and manageable, and then you could enjoy your life doing something you really like, something that would bring you benefits. Instead, you have already wasted all this time on the run, and have no positive energy left for joy and pleasure."

Having said this, the Shaman went quiet. The pause was lengthy and I waited for more. It seemed the Shaman was observing the dancing flames of the fire in front of us, although his eyes were closed. He began to talk again and I thought, at first, he had started a new topic. I was mistaken; it was a broadening of the same philosophy:

"Our fears feed on our thoughts and our inner energy; this is how our fears become real and materialise. In each and every one of us resides something evil. You know that all people, even the most genteel ones, feel anger now and again. Anger is one of the most common human emotions and an example of evil. Anger brings on evil thoughts, and if you fear your own evil thoughts, then this is how you feed them. Alternatively, you can stop focusing on their existence and the evil thoughts will simply fade away. Our thoughts are just like people: if you pay no attention to them, they get offended and leave. If you keep inviting these evil contemplations into your mind, they eventually will eat you from within, although nobody will even notice how rotten and empty your soul has become."

I then asked my very first question: "How is this?"

The Shaman answered. "Inside your soul grows a dark forest full of various inhabitants, think of them as people of different types and characteristics. Some of the forest residents are beautiful, and others are ugly. Some are friendly, while others are frightening. Only you can see them, because they live in your own mind. They are immaterial but you still can decide which ones to nurture. You could encourage and cultivate the wholesome and positive characters, which will beautify your body and enhance your mind. They are very fragile and vulnerable, and while it is difficult, it is important to keep fostering them. You ought to learn how to grow them in the forest of your soul. This forest is equally full of brightly lit valleys and dark foxholes. As the keeper of this forest, you can decide on the balance whether to have more light or more darkness.

Everyone has to manage both the light and dark powers of their mind and soul, but no one gets any help or advice on how to handle them. This is why so few people find enough energy and patience to cultivate the forces of light and warmth."

The bonfire continued to blaze giving out enough heat to keep me warm, while I was sharing its warmth with the Shaman who kindly decided to share his wisdom with me. Slightly bending towards the flames, the Shaman grabbed an armful of dry branches and wood sticks and threw them into the fire. The sparks flew in all directions, the flames shot upwards, as if grateful for the food received from the Shaman. This only lasted a few seconds, and then the fire abruptly diminished as if it was axed at the root.

The Shaman stretched his right hand to the fire soaking up the heat from the flames:

"Do you see this, young man? Look, even the fire cannot accept all this wood that I had thrown in. It cannot digest all this food that I gave with love. Remember how bright the flames were before I added more wood? Remember how they happily danced as soon as they received this huge amount of food? But this only lasted a few minutes, maybe even seconds. Can you see what happened now?"

The pause following this monologue seemed to indicate that the Shaman was expecting my response.

"The flames have died down now." My mouth instantly felt dry. The Shaman had asked me (me!) a question!

Chapter One: The first meeting with a Shaman

"Yes, that is right, young man. The fire had gone down because it got buried under the vast amount of wood that I had thrown in. My intention was to feed the fire in order to allow it to grow brighter and bigger than before. But the opposite happened, the upsurge of the flames only lasted a few moments. If I were throwing one piece of wood after another into the fire, feeding it gradually, it would have kept burning evenly for a long time. It would continue burning steadily just the same. This is because a drip-feed will only support the current level. Likewise, steady support will only keep you afloat where you are, without advancing you any further. Fair enough, it will prevent your fall but it will not help you to grow. When something is given to you it requires no effort on your part. When you receive something easily it is usually not valued enough, and therefore it is soon lost. The true development only comes through an effort."

To confirm these words, the branches that were thrown into the flames finally caught fire and the blaze became bigger and brighter than before. The Shaman fell into the silence, the bonfire burned and the sky was crystal clear, with the stars looking down at me from above with their sharp, glittering eyes.

I sat there trying to understand how it is to have an opportunity to be always connected to the natural beauty of the world. It was so different to see the flames not being confined to the kitchen gas stoves and ovens, not just painted in pictures, or captured in the photographs, or on the TV screen. It was a very enlightening, invigorating and wonderful experience to see not a still picture, but the live fire roaring free. I stretched my arm and almost touched the hot petals of the flames. As I turned my head I saw that my physical body did the same.

The song grew inaudible, only random sounds of the tambourine bells could be heard in the night forest, echoing in the distance. The Shaman continued his quiet speech:

"Learn this life wisdom from the fire, young man. The fire always remains one clean element of Mother Nature. Only fire could not be spoiled by people. Only in the fire will you never find any dirt."

Having said this, the Shaman had gone silent again. His body, which was sitting motionless before, suddenly rose up and he began pounding his feet on the ground. These steps added to the already unusual pattern of the tambourine beats. The Shaman turned around himself several times and started singing again. This time the song wasn't quiet and monotonous but full of energy. I listened, mesmerised by the flow of the music where the sounds were interlaced one with another, the melody flowing deep and powerful as a river.

The tambourine beats and its bells, the sound of the Shaman's feet stomping the ground, his dance, and the song without words – all these presented a certain mysterious sequence of interconnected and inseparable threads, a certain storyline that I could not yet comprehend. It was not dissimilar to how millions of years ago the four elements – fire, earth, water and air – were joined up to create the world we are living in.

The Shaman spoke up again, adding yet another strand into an existing pattern with the sound of his voice:

"Learn from the fire, young man," he repeated. "The fire only has great aims and goals, its targets are always accurate."

Keeping his eyes still closed, the Shaman reached out to the flames:

Chapter One: The first meeting with a Shaman

"Even now, when I locked the flames inside this circle of stones; the fire lives on the inside aiming to escape the confinement and to embrace the whole forest. It is a misconception that fire is evil. Its love is so hot and burning that some may see it as a threat. But the fire is warm and welcoming; it can help to warm your house, to cook your meal. The fire is patient and persistent in its work, it is not to be rushed. You too, young man, should be patient and persistent like this fire.

Set only large goals for yourself and love every single step on the way to your goals. When you aim big you cannot seize your goal in a single step, you need to take many small steps towards it before you will reach your destination. You should love all these little steps and notice every small achievement on the way to your main goal. This will motivate you and drive you to better results, take you to new heights. You need to remember your ultimate goal too, because while taking these baby steps you can simply lose sight of the bigger picture and get absorbed in a meaningless vanity. In order not to fall down, you simply need to keep moving forward."

"What will the fire do after it has burned down the entire forest with its love, then?" I asked, bravely.

"It will do everything it can to continue forward." The Shaman's response sounded like something so obvious I should have known already. "Thus, after the fire had reached its goal of embracing the whole forest, it will advance further."

One question led to another and I asked:

"Then why can't I do the same after I have reached one of my goals?"

The Shaman tossed some more firewood into the flames:

"The fire will make an effort to keep moving forward but it will not be able to, because once the fire has reached the boundaries of the forest it will grow massive and strong. The bigger the fire is, the more food it will need to feed its size. After the forest has burned out, there will be nothing left for the fire to feed on and it will die deprived of 'nourishment' because it does not know how to obtain it beyond the woods. Once you reach your first or second target on the way to your ultimate goal, you will have lost a lot of energy getting there. Do you think it is right to use so much energy to achieve limited results and stop there?"

"Is it not the same with a big goal? Once I am satisfied with the result I will lose the drive to advance, there will be no next 'ultimate goal'?"

The Shaman didn't hesitate a second to respond to my question, he began to talk almost before I finished my question:

"If you make the right choice, your ultimate goal will bring the result that will help you to progress even further, leading to the next goal, towards a greater purpose. All the knowledge and skills you obtained on the way will help you to see the new higher and better target to aim for. However, if your goal was small to begin with it may have been the wrong choice. You will have spent time and energy on the achievement of something not worthy of putting too much effort into it. Having wasted all your strength on this, you will have neither the enthusiasm nor the strength for setting a new objective to aim for."

The song had ended; the spiritual double of the Shaman

Chapter One: The first meeting with a Shaman

finished his speech. Only the slow banging on the tambourine and the unusually loud crackle of the bonfire could now be heard in the otherwise silent night forest. With one question playing on my mind, I feared the worst, and I could not resist asking:

"What if I die before reaching my main goal, my life's purpose?"

"You seem to have already forgotten my words," the Shaman didn't open his eyes but his voice sounded reproachful. Even the tambourine beats appeared dissatisfied with my challenge. "You must love your path regardless, every single step of it. To build something significant is possible only if you are sincere about it; you need to dedicate your mind and soul to it, and also your heart. Even if your life journey will end before your purpose is completed, it will have been filled with love."

"But then why is there so much evil in the world?" I persisted.

"Because evil grows much faster than good. You need to work hard on keeping the good alive; you need to be patient, consistent and persistent in this work. This is not an easy task and you need to learn how to master it. The forest of your soul is already inhabited and it is up to you how the inhabitants will turn out, good or evil. No effort is required to grow evil, but the good will only exist if there is enough room for them. If your forest is already full of evil thoughts you will need to do extra work to make space for the good ones. Like the artfully landscaped parks and gardens can become overgrown with weeds, without care your soul's forest can become a refuge for evil."

"But the woodland can be cleared and tidied up again?" I asked again.

"Sadly, no. When the forest is too overgrown no garden surgeon can help. Only a bushfire can clear up all the evil. Only the bushfire will wipe it off clean."

"But the fire doesn't clean anything; it burns all that happens to be in its way!" I exclaimed.

"No, not exactly. Burning is an act of cleaning too," the Shaman contradicted me, speaking slowly and quietly and gently rocking his body to the rhythm of his tambourine. "The fire clears the ground of everything. True, it destroys both evil and good at the same time, preparing the ground for a new fresh forest. But the good was not strong enough to overtake the evil in the first place, which means it was worthless. You, as the keeper of the forest, were responsible for the balance between evil and good forces. If you did not succeed in cleansing your soul and ridding it of evil, now it is time to create a new forest filled only with the positive thoughts. You are responsible for keeping it clean and in good condition, you and only you can make the new forest better than the forest that had been growing there before."

Silence ensued. The Shaman opened his eyes and made a throaty sound. Instantly, the magic surrounding me was gone.

✳✳✳

I sat on the rough wooden log. Across from me, looking through the transparent flames, I could see the figure of the Shaman. Wind of the North had stopped singing, he was no longer rocking his body, his lips didn't move. He looked like a big ruffled up owl sitting on a branch at the top of the tree, observing everything with its big round yellow eyes.

The Shaman continued to sit silently watching me, closely

examining my face. He looked at me intently, evidently searching for some signs in my face, which would be visible only to him. Signs of what – of my understanding? Acknowledgement? Agreement? By now I also felt relaxed and unreservedly scrutinised the Shaman's face. His old skin was dark and lined, looking rather like the bark of a hundred year old tree, perhaps an ancient oak or a cedar tree that had stood against foul weather and survived many storms.

Wind of the North leaned forward and lifted another twig from the pile of firewood on the ground. He looked into my eyes once more and threw the twig into the fire. The sparks shot up to the sky and the bonfire suddenly became unbearably bright, seeming to shield the entire world with its flames… when my eyes were again able to see and distinguish my surroundings, everything had disappeared – the Shaman, the fire, the logs we sat on. Everything was gone. Now I could only see an unfriendly, damp and dark forest around me, and a narrow foot trail that I needed to take, in order to lead myself home.

Chapter Two
The song of Four Elements

Feeling inspired by my first conversation with the Shaman called Wind of the North, I tried, time and time again, to make another 'appointment' with this old wise man. I am not quite sure how to describe my first meeting with him. Perhaps, the closest analogy would be to a therapy session. Meeting with a person who is there for you, even if only for a limited time – you can tell them anything and everything that is bothering you, describe all your problems, relay to them all the worries and concerns that are keeping you awake at night.

This therapist, of course, would have to be a certified specialist, a professional counsellor. Since we think our problems are the most complex and difficult to resolve then only the most qualified expert could possibly deal with

Chapter Two: The song of Four Elements

them. The therapist would listen and in ten minutes or so would be able to put each of your problems into perspective and offer a solution on how to fix them all. After this sorting out exercise, you would see that all your extremely complex problems were not that irresolvable after all, and there are over a thousand solutions available. Then you would consider your life sorted, or so it would seem until you were on your own again, face to face with those very concerns and fears, and not a therapist in sight.

But going back to my conversation with the Shaman, I now understood why it is so important for everyone to be able to tap into his inner 'shaman' whose advice is available any time of night or day, regardless of where we are, and without any need for a therapist. I enjoyed my first meeting with my shaman so much that every day I had been trying to find a way of seeing him again, but all my attempts were unsuccessful. It appeared that my wise counsellor deliberately decided to give me a breather, as if to give me time to absorb and digest all the wisdom that he shared with me. Of course, I cannot be sure of that but I would like to believe this is the reason why, at least at first, I had no success in finding him.

People always believe in what suits them best, and what they feel comfortable to accept. They always try to find a good reason for why things happen or don't happen in a certain way. Like everyone else, I choose to believe my own explanation. The alternative might have meant my meeting with Wind of the North was purely coincidental, and that I should not hold my hopes up high to see this wise man again.

On the day when I was finally able to get through the barriers of my unconscious, I was quite angry with a few people, with valid reason. Perhaps, the level and the strength of my anger, the energy of my feelings and my passion, gave me a push to reach out to the Shaman. Perhaps, not. Perhaps, all of it was only my imagination, together with a desire to believe I had made it happen. Perhaps, there was no push at all, and nothing that happened next was the result of my trying. Perhaps, the Shaman living in the depth of my soul and my mind had sensed how disturbed I was and had come along to help. Perhaps, he had decided to give me a warning, a lesson, and another piece of invaluable advice.

✳✳✳

Going by the fact that the second conversation with the Shaman was rather short, I can only assume I was not ready for all the wisdom and the Shaman simply stopped me from making any rushed decisions and actions.

Soon enough, I found myself in the same forest but this time I somehow got there without the help of a Jeep driver. I could see again that barely visible foot trail taking me into the depths of the forest, and the stars watching over me from above. Again, I felt the strange sensation of someone invisible being present. Here was that same old tree, the root of which I had slipped and tripped over the last time, and even though I saw it again this time, I again stumbled upon it. I moved the prickly fir tree branch out of the way with my bare hand, feeling its roughness.

I saw the same valley in front of me. I can't even call it a valley, but rather a clearing where the forest opened to leave room for the log, the fire, and the Shaman. I could see that familiar log I previously used as a bench, with the Shaman sitting opposite it, across the fire. He was expecting me, his song already strong and his spirit already detached from his

Chapter Two: The song of Four Elements

physical body. I could hear all four elements of nature in his song – fire, air, water and earth. Yet I could hear more than that this time, something else in his song that was very small, and very discreet. This little something reminded me of random water drops, when the spring storm is just beginning. It reminded me of the soft yet powerful blow of the wind when the hurricane begins. Once the hurricane gains its full power it will rip the roofs of houses and move large rocks from the mountain peaks. Until it reaches the level of its full force you cannot tell how powerful the hurricane is going to be. Likewise, this little 'something' in the Shaman's song had not yet fully formed, I could only just sense it, rather than hear it. Yet, somehow, I was already confident that I would shortly recognise what it was.

The Shaman began to speak without any greeting or small talk. Without any preamble, he continued as if we had never parted, and he had never stopped his lecture:

"When a person is angry he is possessed with the malice that stops him from living his own life. The angrier he gets, the more this anger grips his soul," I could detect a disappointment in the Shaman's voice. "When you allow your anger to take over, you cannot think of anything else except your own bitterness, and of the person who awoke these feelings in you. This only means that the person who caused you emotional pain has already won. He invaded your life through making you angry. The longer you stay angry, the more angry and sad you will get. The winner has entered that 'forest' of your soul and set up his own fire in there, but you are the only person who can extinguish that fire. It depends solely on you whether that fire will continue burning like this one."

"Could you explain please?" I found the courage to ask the Shaman for clarification. "Continue burning like the fire in this fireplace?"

"Burning, like this one," repeated the Shaman as if he hasn't heard my question but simply elaborated on the thought – "I have no power over this fire but I have control over it. This fire always lights up in the same place and I keep watch over it, to make sure it does not come out of its stone circle, to make sure it does not expand to take over the whole forest."

I understood these words were related directly to my feelings of anger, and that their design and purpose was to make me see and understand what anger could do to me, how it could destroy my life. The beats of the tambourine echoed in the silence of the night forest. From time to time, these monotonous beats were intercepted by the words from the Shaman's song, the words, which I still could not make out, since the song was sung in a language unfamiliar to me. Even though I could not make any sense of the words, the tone of them seemed as if the Shaman had reprimanded me for something, and that Mother Nature was not only listening, but also watching and waiting for my response, whether I understood the words spoken to me, or if they simply passed me by.

"A man possessed by his anger exists unconsciously," said the Shaman, and his words sounded sharp and snappy. The subject was clearly unpleasant and the Shaman seemed to have to force himself to continue on this topic. Perhaps, he was hoping that if he repeated it enough times his message would finally hit home, and would help me to deal with, and overcome, my anger. "An angry individual doesn't live in the moment; he lives in the past infected by his bitter feelings of

Chapter Two: The song of Four Elements

upset. He doesn't live his own life but the life designed for him by his offender. He constantly follows the person who upset him or made him jealous or envious.

An angry individual follows closely in the footsteps of another person's life forgetting to live his own. Your own life ceases to exist and becomes mere survival when you begin taking more interest in someone else's life than in your own, especially (!) when the person in question is the one towards whom you feel the anger and even the hate. That anger is eating you from within, it is burning you from the inside out, consuming all the good feelings and thoughts you had."

Then again, there was a short silence, as if the Shaman was giving me some time to reflect on what he had just said:

"I am comparing your anger with the forest fire. Do you understand why? Because your abuser has entered your soul's forest. Perhaps you have let him in yourself. Maybe you opened the door to your soul and mind to your abuser because you trusted and believed they were a friend but they betrayed you. Or, maybe you have simply let your defences fall. Perhaps the barrier you have built to protect your soul's forest from strangers is not strong enough to protect your sensitive and vulnerable thoughts and feelings. If that fence has fallen down, anyone can now trespass through your soul, traipsing in their dirty boots over the flowers, leaving a lot of mud there, and lighting up their own fire in your forest where an entry was prohibited. As I said, you have the power to extinguish that fire and clear up the mud. You must watch over this fire and decide how to take control over it."

"You have two options now. First, you can simply stop feeding this fire with your angry feelings; this will stop the fire getting any bigger. In this case, the stranger's fire already burning in the midst of your soul will lessen and eventually die down completely, because it will be completely deprived of fuel. Where the fire had been burning, there will be a burnt-out area, which will be overgrown by the moss or new grass.

The other option is, you take control over the fire and feed it with your negative feelings. In this case the fire will keep burning for a long time; it will keep consuming the energy that could have otherwise been used for success, rather than self-destruction. This fire will die down too, eventually, but it will take a long time, and the spot where it had been will be completely scorched and no vegetation will be able to grow in that place for a long, long time."

The Shaman fell silent again as if the picture he painted himself had horrified him. Even his song had stopped, and the tambourine beats sounded somewhat lost and lonely, suggesting sadness and sorrow:

"This is not the worst, though. The worst happens when a person is unable to control the fire. The fire becomes wild, deadly and gruesome in its might. Such a fire burns everything in its way. The stones crack, the birds fall down from the sky screaming in pain and die from the heat before their burned bodies hit the ground. There is no salvation from such a fire. It destroys everything because it is filled not with love but hatred. The earth is left charred and nothing can survive this inferno. Its sole purpose is to burn all the living; its flames are not cleansing but deadly and evil. Your soul's forest cannot cope and fight against this firestorm; it needs help that only you can give. While the flames are only gaining strength, a healthy heavy rain can stop them, but if

Chapter Two: The song of Four Elements

the weather is dry the fire will grow fast and spread wide, and it will be necessary to call the fire fighters."

"But time, it heals everything, right?" I was asking for reassurance, but the Shaman only shook his head.

"Time never heals anything. Time is not a pill that you can take three times a day to treat the disease or to ease the symptoms. Time only delays the decision. It pushes away the pain, creating the distance between you and the solution. Over time, we simply learn to live with the pain that still never goes away."

"But with time, even infertile soil will get green. With time, the metal will rust. Time affects everything." I was not going to give up easily.

"It is not time that does this, my friend. It is nature," the Shaman indicated with his hand pointing out to the woods around us. "Nature is essentially a huge living organism, and like any living organic body it has its own healing resources to heal wounds caused by us, by people. The wounds we create in our hectic pursuit of power and wealth. Our cities are like huge tumours on the body of nature. It is hardly surprising that once people leave, nature begins its self-healing process. Nonetheless, if you want your wounds to heal more quickly you should not put your reliance only on nature, because it is busy with other things. You need to help nature; you need to help time."

"You need to fertilise that scorched land to help new growth, sow new fresh seeds of good. The wounds in your soul will heal too, because what is left after the fire? The ashes are left, and they are fertiliser for the soil. Any good seeds that you sow there will be kept warm by the blanket of ashes left after that vicious fire. These ashes now will be protecting the new young seeds from the most severe frost and keeping them moist even during the driest of summers."

The silence fell again. The continuous beats of the tambourine had not stopped, but seemed to have moved away and become a dull background sound. The voice of the wind whistling through the treetops, along with the other sounds of the forest, such as the creaking of the branches bending in the wind sounding like a large bird flapping its wings, came to the forefront of my hearing. A city dweller cannot even imagine all these whispers of the night forest, and if they happen to be in the forest at night, they will perceive all these sounds as threatening, hostile and frightening. An experienced forest keeper can easily distinguish between the dangerous and friendly sounds; he knows how to avoid the former and to exploit the latter. He knows how to turn the danger to his own advantage. Only a person who knows nature well can accept that in it, there is never an absolute silence.

I thought, "We, the residents of big cities, forgot these sounds long ago, or perhaps we never even knew them." Exhausted from the never-ending noise, from the buzz and cacophony of the cities, from overcrowded houses, we have forgotten there is never an absolute silence in nature. An absolute silence is equal to death, and therefore impossible to hear while we are alive. In nature, everything has sounds, and these sounds are melody. The music of the wind, the sound of the falling water drops, the whisper of the rustling grass and even the sound of footsteps in the crispy crust of deep snow – all this is nature's music. All this is the music of life and it cannot be taken over by the silence of death, unless we allow it.

Chapter Two: The song of Four Elements

I felt really grateful for that one moment of silence, during which I had a chance to remember this. Just one minute of silence gave me an opportunity to hear all that music of life again.

※※※

The conversation was over. Peace and quiet ensued. In front of me, gleaming in the moonlight, was again the foot trail that would lead me through the forest. What should I do? Go back to my life, or turn to the Shaman still sitting by his fire and ask him some more questions in the hope that this wise old man would give me more advice, and share more knowledge?

Something had stopped me from turning to the Shaman again, though. The conversation was clearly over, and there must have been a reason why at our first meeting the Shaman had demonstrated how too much firewood could destroy a fire. Perhaps, he was showing me what could happen to my mind if I was given too much information while unprepared for it.

"Perhaps, I should not rush things," I said out loud. "Everything in its time, and time for everything."

Making this statement to myself helped me to reach a decision, and I began to make my way back home with newly found confidence.

Chapter Three
A candle in the dark

To my delight, soon after our second meeting, the Shaman agreed to meet me again for another discussion, or rather, another session of questions and answers. Our third meeting occurred shortly before my birthday and it felt like this meeting was a birthday gift – a gift I made to myself, or perhaps a gift from the Shaman himself, or some other, higher force.

I was feeling rather down at the time. I am not alone in this. It so often happens that many people feel quite sad during holiday season or a day of celebration. More than that, when a person feels lonely in their life in general, or if they are alone only during the time of the celebration, that same celebration usually turns into a misery instead. These special moments become a catalyst for sadness, highlighting

Chapter Three: A candle in the dark

the feelings of loneliness gripping the human soul and heart with cold fingers.

Now, after some time had passed, I have come to believe that these feelings of sadness and loneliness set the direction of our conversation that day. Being alone is not the same as feeling lonely. The solitude is a choice, the loneliness is not.

"What do I do about my loneliness, how do I live with it?" I asked this question expecting Wind of the North to give me a defined and solid answer, indeed, to offer the solution.

The Shaman sat opposite me on another side of his fireplace that was again enclosed in a rough circle made from the stones. His eyes were closed, the eyelids trembled slightly but the Shaman did not open them. He began talking in a whisper, and his words flowed toward me as slowly as the rising tide. This tidal wave of wisdom was endless and limitless like the water in the ocean, and it was solid like the rocks guarding the most intimate secrets of the sea.

When I began to fear being crushed by the amount of knowledge that was about to fall upon me from even his whisper, the Shaman spoke in a loud voice and his speech silenced the whisper of his eerie double sitting right beside his body on the log.

"When you feel lonely just light up a candle. Take any candle, small or large, be it one with a pleasant fragrance, or a simple plain one. It doesn't matter what kind of candle you choose or happen to have to hand. Just light that candle. Even though the flame might be small, and seems insignificant, that little fire is alive."

As if to support his words by a visual demonstration, the Shaman reached for some firewood. He took out a crooked dry twig from a pile of brushwood and threw it into a bonfire. The fire sparkled and the Shaman traced them with his eyes from under lowered eyelids. Then he continued his speech:

"Fire has been with people for many years, long before humanity itself understood it. Fire was keeping people warm; from the dawn of human history it was defending them from the dangers of the wild. When you feel lonely just light up a candle and let the fire into your home, and into your life.

Remember, fire is a living thing; it burns and breathes, unlike the electric light, which only gives out artificial light."

The Shaman suddenly made a sweeping movement with his hands as if covering the burning fire with something, the fire went out and darkness descended upon us. I have never seen a bonfire go out so fast. I could not detect even any glimmering as it cooled down; the fire simply disappeared as if it had been switched off! The Shaman let me feel the darkness as if it was something tangible rather than a mere absence of light. He then produced a candle which he took out somewhere from behind his back, and surprisingly the candle was already burning.

"There is no such darkness that cannot be penetrated and lit up by the single flame of a candle. This small red tongue of a flame living on a short wick is always warm and welcoming, ready to share its light and warmth with you at any time during the cold winter months and in the darkness of rainy and wet autumn nights."

Another movement with his hands and the Shaman took off the invisible blanket from the bonfire. The flames once again

Chapter Three: A candle in the dark

danced happily on the charred firewood in the middle of the fireplace. The Shaman's voice was strong and urgent, it seemed he wanted to convey his words to the very core of my mind. He spoke with such knowledge it embedded into my memory, and has remained with me forever.

"Nowadays people have put a fence around them and become isolated from nature. People hide behind the concrete walls of their houses and apartments. As if this isolation was not enough for people, they have started distancing themselves not only from nature but also from each other, from their own families and friends. People are now hiding behind the blue flickering screens of their computers, living their lives in the artificial light of electric lamps. It is hardly surprising that they feel lonely more often now; but they try to escape from being alone in the wrong way. In their search for an exit from this self-created loneliness, people get deeper and deeper into the maze of the internet, hoping in there to find values such as human companionship, friendship, and even love. Sadly, they only get tangled up in that web without even realising it. People do not seem to understand, or simply refuse to acknowledge, that this 'web' is like a cobweb, linking people together but not doing much else. Each individual attached to this cobweb remains alone, and as lonely as before."

"Light a candle, don't let that feeling of loneliness settle down in your soul and become a part of you!" These words the Shaman said with his eyes wide open. I expected that the meeting would end there and then, as it had happened before. But, apparently, the Shaman thought differently. He obviously had not said everything he intended to share with me. The flames shot up skywards under his gaze as if a sudden gust of wind had blown them; the Shaman lowered his eyelids and began his next song.

The words of his song were tearing from his lips, flying to the heavens above, but before reaching the sky they hovered, rising above the canopy of the forest, and fell down in a shower of thousands of stars. Following this rain of stars with my eyes, I then looked at the Shaman. He was singing, the same tambourine appeared in his hands again, its beats accompanying the song. I still couldn't make out any words, or didn't understand the language. But this time I felt able to work out all five components of the melody.

Just like last time, there were four elements in his song – fire, earth, water and air. I remembered there was the fifth element weaving itself into the song and joining all other four elements, completing the fine pattern and creating the whole picture. This fifth element was now strong, and competing with the other four. The fire was giving out warmth, but the realisation had sent shivers down my back. I understood what the fifth element was – it was human. The man himself, by the strength of a human spirit, his thought and creativity, created this power of a human.

The song resonating and echoing in the forest had carried a reflection of all the energy of the planet. First, at my first meeting with the Shaman, his song only included four elements because he was singing about ancient times when the human mind was not yet fully developed. In our second conversation the fifth component was only emerging, making its way to the surface through the maze of the other four elements. The four elements were in harmony, and at the same time in competition with one another; it was difficult to distinguish the fifth, the human part.

Chapter Three: A candle in the dark

This time, the song was complete and fell down on me as the rain of words, or, as I had visualized it, the rain of stars. It was falling upon us, upon the forest around us. This time, all five components of the song were equal and strong. Did I play any part in creating this new pattern, its harmony and flow? The Shaman seemed to have sensed that I understood the meaning of his song, and his voice gradually tailed off. Silence ensued. I then thought, if this song is now complete then what songs will the Shaman sing the next time we meet? Is there going to be a next time?

"May I ask a question? Or is it better I say nothing?" I addressed my words to both the Shaman, and the fire burning in front of us.

The song had finished, the Shaman parted his lips slowly and said:

"You can ask, young man. More than that, you should ask. But you should only talk if you are true to your words, if your actions reflect what you say. When your words become muddled up, when you feel a stranger to your own thoughts, words and actions, you will have to stop talking."

"Have to stop? For how long?" I was confused. Such a simple statement, yet I could not comprehend.

The Shaman looked surprised by my question but responded anyway:

"For as long as it is necessary, or until such time when your actions will align with your thoughts and words. It is important for a person to speak up, just as it is important to dream. Do not be afraid to dream, it gives you strength. Your dreams give you wings; they drive you forward to the realisation of your plans. But you mustn't forget that dreams are different from plans. Plans should have actions and steps for their achievement, but dreams may remain dreams forever, and never become a reality.

You can structure your plan of actions, but you can dream about something unrealistic, fantasise like children do. Believe in your dream, it is important. If you believe in your dream then your dream will believe in you too! Even during the most difficult moments of your life, your dreams can help you retain sincerity, the purity of thoughts. They will help you to retain that inner child who lives in your mind, free of evil. Only by remaining a child on the inside, will you be able to keep your mind flexible, to bend the principles and go beyond them, to create new values, to think outside the box. Only a child-like mind is capable of creation and of being spontaneous. This requires some effort on your part, not to slip into the mould of a stereotypical adult existing in the constraints of a modern world and its strict rules and frames.

People who don't know how to dream are disadvantaged; perhaps they can even be called deprived, or incapacitated. Just as some people are unable to walk, or talk, or cannot see – they miss something in life. Those unable to dream are also missing out in a significant way. There is a reason why people dream, it is the only way forward. It was dreams that drove the explorers to their great discoveries, drove the scientists to innovations. The pilots were able to conquer the sky only because people have always dreamed of flying, and that dream intensified with each generation of dreamers.

There is no need to be embarrassed by your dreams, just because you worry that someone may think them childish or stupid. This is the nature of the dream – it CAN be silly

Chapter Three: A candle in the dark

and unrealistic, until you make a plan for how to achieve that dream. Then nobody will be laughing. You must also remember to never judge another person's dream," the Shaman had raised his voice, "your dreams keep you going, they help you live your life, to improve and grow. Your dreams are your aspirations that take you higher. In this cruel and demanding world of actions you must cherish your dreams and appreciate everything you already have. This will help you to go through life and make it enjoyable.

Never turn your back on anything that helps you to get closer to your goals, whether it is a person, a thought or belief, or a philosophy. A person only needs a few warm and friendly words to feel better and comfortable. Just a few words can make a big difference between mental suffering and inspiration. There are also people who need a lengthy conversation to help ease their anguish and to calm down. We are all different, we dream differently and about different things. Some dreams may look shallow, others may seem too grand, but no one should feel embarrassed by their dreams. We also have different opinions and that's OK. You should never feel obliged to think the same as others."

After a short pause in his powerful and emotional monologue, the Shaman began his song again. The melody of his song was quiet and peaceful. It was a while before he started to speak. He did not change the subject, but continued talking about importance of dreams:

"When a person mentally revisits his dreams again and again, his mind is at rest. His mind is abstracted from the reality. Unfortunately, the reality is often far from perfect and the time spent dreaming helps to give the brain some rest, to relax, to chill out.

It is important to learn to use your unconscious mind when you are dreaming. You must learn to not simply dream seeing pictures of what it will be like if your dream comes true, but also look for ways of realising this dream, to look for key pointers that will turn your dream into a goal and push you towards it. Your goal could be anything, it could be either intellectual knowledge or skills (an academic title, for example), or something more tangible (the level of your earnings). Never refuse help offered to you when you are working towards your goal, never turn away from those willing to assist you, never ignore even the smallest things that can be useful on your path to success."

A silence followed this speech, which emphasised the importance of the Shaman's next words:

"You must be prepared for the fact that while on your path, you will also be met with much indifference. People will look into your eyes, seemingly understanding and agreeing, even supporting you. But behind your back they might laugh or feel skeptical about you or your dreams and ideas. These people don't really care about you or your words, your thoughts, ideas, concerns and worries. They are indifferent. This is neither good nor bad; it is what it is, simply accept it. Perhaps, some people will eventually grow to understand and associate, and even sympathise with you. But this is unlikely. Don't hold your breath, and forget about it. Just move on, surround yourself with others who are supportive or, at the very least, tolerant and understanding.

A very small percentage of people in your life will sincerely want to help you without an ulterior motive. Be careful not to lose them, keep them safe, and look after them more than you look after your wallet. Don't classify them, don't label them. It doesn't matter whether their help is physical, material, or simply some words of support during your time of despair. It often happens that a kind word said in a timely manner and with sincerity brings about the positive energy that protects your faith, your belief, your confidence and your self-respect.

The mere knowledge that your phone book contains the number of a person whom you can always call, any time of day or night, with whom you can share your problems, reveal your soul's pain, is enough. It is enough to give you comfort and reassurance; it is enough to lighten up your load and to light up your darkness. Sometimes, it is not even necessary to make that phone call, simply knowing such a person exists may be sufficient. But you should also be prepared for the fact that many people will be rather displeased because you are advancing to your goal. This is often because they got stuck on the way to their own goals, and the deeper they are rooted on the spot without going forward the stronger will be their criticism of you, of your successes. The more disapproving they are, the more dirt they will pour over you, gossiping and talking behind your back.

Unfortunately, there are more of such negative people in the world than those who will genuinely be proud of your achievements and support you. Learn how to ignore them. If you intend to grow and rise higher, you will need to grow thick skinned, and protect yourself from their attacks. You must build immunity against their accusations, their envy and jealousy. You need to be strong to protect your heart and soul from those predators, to keep your thoughts and dreams pure. If you let your defences down your heart and soul will be open to all the cruelty your enemies have in store for you. Keep your armour strong and under your control, don't allow anyone to weaken you, to invade the forest of your soul and light up their own fire in there. Resilience is one word you must not only remember, but also learn to use."

Having said that, the Shaman opened his eyes and looked at me. His song had stopped. The flames shot upwards and the fire instantly grew so large, it completely hid the Shaman from me. The stars were so close that I felt like I could reach them, I only needed to stretch my arm and – here! – I could pick up a star from the sky, touch it, roll it in my hands, and then put it back where it belonged…

✷✷✷

When the conversation was over, I again stood alone on the same foot trail in the forest. No log, no fire, not even any charcoal where the fire had been burning. With sadness, I sighed. Every time after seeing the Shaman and having these conversations, I felt sad and lonely, even more lonely than before. All my feelings were emphasised and amplified. Whatever I felt before seeing the Shaman, I felt more acutely after. The reason for this, perhaps, was that the magic had dispersed and, once again, I had to return to reality, to the familiar world. I am not saying this world is bad, but I cannot turn a blind eye to how cruel it can be without miracles and magic.

Chapter Four
Stepping into the unknown

The winter had arrived with its long dark evenings and frosty Siberian nights. During the winter months, all I wanted to do was go to bed and go into hibernation, like a bear. It was a long time since my last meeting with the Shaman, or at least this was how it seemed to me. Hence, it was not surprising that my desire to see him was getting stronger and stronger, and I was spending a lot of time thinking about how I could get through to him again. I always thought about it in the evenings. One cold December evening, I finally succeeded.

Just like the last few times, I once again found myself in the middle of the same foot trail leading into the midst of the thick dark forest. The darkness of the night taiga surrounded me again, and the silence was so profound it was deafening, yet full of the hidden sounds of Mother Nature. The sky looked especially bright that night, with more stars visible than ever.

Standing on the footpath I suddenly thought – who made this path? How did it appear? No one lived here, I knew that for sure. No one ever walked this path either, because I knew Wind of the North was my personal 'adviser'. He may have been meeting me by the fire in the middle of this Siberian taiga, but I now also knew that this deep thick forest was, in fact, inside my soul, and no one else could have ever walked that path because it was my path! Thinking that, I bent to look closer at the ground. The stars were shining so brightly I could see the footpath clearly, and it became obvious people's shoes didn't make the path. The thought was disconcerting, and I shivered, yet I shrugged it off and continued on my way. Whoever made this narrow road for me, person or not, the only way for me was forward. After having tried so hard to see the Shaman again, I was not going to miss our meeting.

"This is you, human nature!" I muttered quietly. "First you want something so badly you can't think of anything else at all. Then something distracts you, sometimes something absolutely trivial and unimportant, that nevertheless affects you so much you start thinking about it all the time. Then you begin to doubt and even think whether you wanted that something at all." This kind of self-analysis is not typical for me; I may have already fallen under the spell of my imminent meeting with the Shaman.

I don't know whether the Shaman had been watching me and reading my thoughts. If so, it was through his own mystical ways he had guessed what I was thinking about, for he began

Chapter Four: Stepping into the unknown

his talk exactly on the subject bothering me. Be that as it may, his speech seemed an extension of my thinking. As soon as our spectral counterparts parted from our bodies and sat opposite each other the Shaman began his song. The song was quiet enough for me to be able to hear and distinguish every word his eerie body was saying.

"Stepping into the unknown is always a bit scary. Some do it with joy, and some never summon their strength, they just do not have the gumption to get out of their comfort zone and into unknown territory, preferring the limited freedom they have to a free flow. Imagine a log drifting down the river. It is free in a way that it is not tied to a bay or a lock; it floats on the water surface moving forward with the stream. But its course is predetermined by the river – by its direction, by the speed of the water flow, and is confined within the boundaries of the riverbank. The log cannot change its speed by its own accord: it can only match the water current. If there is a bend in the river the log can turn too, but only if the river width allows. If the log is too long for the river width, or too heavy for the water speed, it could miss the turn and will be thrown onto the shore. It will then stay there until the next spring in the hope that rising water will pick it up again and pull it back into the current so it can continue moving."

Hearing this, my eyebrows shot up in surprise. I still am sure that the Shaman was somehow closely monitoring my reaction to his words all the time. He continued:

"People and their behaviour can be compared to the trees and bushes. The trees are striving to grow, stretching their trunks high up towards the sun. Likewise, some people, like the trees, grow up to new heights. But other people are like the bushes. The bushes can grow thick and wide, they can spread on the ground but don't aim high. They are comfortable as they are, staying close to the ground. There are people like that too, they do not wish to grow and do not aspire to any heights. The bushes are happy with the convenience of spreading their roots and branches wide – this way they can obtain enough sunlight if they cover a wider surface. They receive enough nutrients from the soil; they don't need to grow tall. However, there are bushes like the fern that can evolve, grow bigger and taller, and eventually they grow as tall as trees. People, too, can come out of their comfort zones and grow, whether by choice, or because they are forced to do so by circumstances."

The Shaman fell silent, giving me time to digest this unusual statement. The sound of his song was muffled and I couldn't distinguish all the individual elements. Perhaps, the time for a new song had not yet come. But perhaps, the time of the old song had expired as well.

The stars were looking at me from above, silently, without any emotion. They just looked at me with interest. Don't get me wrong, I understand that their interest was not my merit; it was brought upon me by the Shaman. But I suddenly felt as if I were on the stage of some school drama play.

The Shaman must have sensed my self-consciousness and continued his speech breaking the spell:

"It is commonly understood that the tree should live and grow in the forest surrounded by other trees, not amongst the bushes. If a tree will grow in the middle of the bushes, the bushes will eventually smother and kill its roots. The bushes need a lot of soil, moisture and nutrients, they will take it all

Chapter Four: Stepping into the unknown

from the earth and there won't be enough left for the tree. The bushes will spread their roots wide through the ground, intertwining themselves with the roots of the tree. While the bushes may be not as tall and don't have trunks as thick and strong as the tree, their roots are by no means weaker, and the sheer amount of them can kill the tree. When this happens, it is time to uproot and move on, move into the forest where other trees grow. In this case, it's time to think of 'walking trees' that tear their roots out from the land and move into the forest to join other trees.

Other trees in the forest are supportive of each other, each tree only taking as many nutrients from the soil as it needs. Smaller trees grow near the big and strong ones; they can lean on their stronger brothers and feel protected. However, if a tree continued growing in the bush land it would not get any support, but would be using all its strength to survive rather than grow. It would have to face hard winds on its own, not being shielded by the forest. The surrounding bushes would cling to the tree, and would only make it more difficult for the tree to keep standing.

It will be much easier for a young tree to survive in the middle of the high forest, amongst strong giant trees. The young tree can look up to the old ones for an inspiration, using them as role models for how to grow tall and strong. Growing amongst other trees, the young tree will not be threatened by the branches and the roots of numerous bushes, restricting its growth. Pine forests reach up to the skies, they grow on pristine soil and you will not see any bushes around to hinder the growth and prosperity of the pines. Occasionally, a beautiful flower can grow on the rotten soil but this is extremely rare. There is no need to make things difficult and use bad soil when you can sow the seeds into a groomed flower bed. It is the same with trees, why struggle amongst the bushes when there is plenty of room in the forest?"

I looked around with curiosity, hoping to better explore the forest around me. However, I did not have time. The Shaman had barely finished talking when the sounds of the tambourine became so loud that even the moon hid behind the cloud, as if frightened by these powerful beats. The darkness descended upon the forest. Except for the circle of light from the flames, some shadows, and the disproportionately shaped hearth, nothing else was visible. Everything beyond that small circle of light was in complete darkness, as if this were a solar eclipse. Yet, this darkness was breathing, and quietly pulsating with life.

Taking a deep breath, the Shaman began a new song, and at the same instant, his spiritual double spoke:

"Every evening we wrap ourselves in a blanket, hoping that tomorrow morning we will wake, suddenly turned into butterflies. However, this will not happen, not tomorrow, not the day after, and not ever. Why, you would ask? Because you cannot keep thinking – maybe today, maybe tomorrow, maybe some time later in the future I will become what I want to be. There is no tomorrow in today's world. While you remember the past and dream about the future, you only live in the moment. Whatever you intend to do should be done today, and today only. For without today, there is no tomorrow.

Butterflies are born as caterpillars. To turn into a butterfly, a caterpillar has to do enormous work and it has to do it

Chapter Four: Stepping into the unknown

today, now, this very minute. Because the life of a butterfly is short, and if the caterpillar doesn't persist it will never turn into a butterfly, but will die a caterpillar. It is a difficult job to accumulate the necessary amount of nutrients, to spin yourself into a cocoon, and then to completely rebuild your body. But if a caterpillar can summon up enough strength for this, so can a human. Whatever it is you want to do, it must start today.

If a caterpillar fails to work on its regeneration and evolution it will never become a beautiful butterfly. But people in their infinite laziness forget that nothing in the world happens by itself, suddenly. Everything is preceded by something, by a process that leads to the final result. If we don't see the work behind the scenes it doesn't mean the work is not happening. There are two ways of getting the result. One, do all the background work yourself. It is hard, time-consuming, tedious, and full of stumbles and failures on the way. But it is one sure way the necessary work will get done. Another way is to delegate, to get somebody else to do the work. This way, you won't have much control over how it's done, and no guarantee it will get done in time and the way you want it. In any case, it is useful to remember that the result may not be exactly as you envisaged. It is more likely that you will get the result you want if you do the work yourself."

Wind of the North took a deep breath in:

"Imagine the caterpillar delegating the work it needs to do in order to regenerate and evolve. Is that possible? Of course not. But even if a miracle happened and it were possible, the result wouldn't be the same as it would be if the caterpillar did all the regeneration work itself. Yes, the butterfly still could be beautiful, but all its beauty would be only superficial. The coloured patterned wings would not be real, but like stencilled colours on a plain grey surface. It might look beautiful for a short while, but then all the colours would fade. To become beautiful on the outside one must first be beautiful on the inside; otherwise the ugly core will eventually show. Do not forget that all beauty should come from within, because the essence of nature is such that multicolour painted to hide something will wash off, and the blank canvas of your inner world will resurface."

After these words, the Shaman did something I did not expect. He bent down and picked up one twig from the heap of brushwood, and threw it over to me. This clearly was an indication that I should throw it into the fire. Not without some trepidation, this was exactly what I did.

When the sparks from the fire consuming the wood thrown by me dispersed, the Shaman continued on:

"Remember, my friend, we are all responsible for our loved ones. We may be not solely responsible, but the responsibility is shared. Our loved ones may purposely, or unintentionally, hurt us, but we are still responsible for them. Unfortunately, people suffer and pay the price for their sins and mistakes, worse still, they are often held liable for the mistakes of others. Choose carefully whom you love, young man. Notice the people around you, your closest and dear ones, and your friends. Are they worthy of your suffering, of your being accountable for their blunders? Do they deserve your affection and your care? People, like the trees in the forest, should surround themselves with others similar to them. Just as the tree will struggle to grow amongst many weeds and shrubs, so will people be held back by others."

Chapter Four: Stepping into the unknown

A weak-spirited person always tries to find a reason for their weakness, to justify their cowardice, to explain their stupidity. In reality there is no reason, no justification, no explanation – only an excuse, and a poor excuse for that matter. Just like the bushes getting shelter from the storm behind the trunks of large trees or stone boulders, so people try to hide from the truth. The strong trees stand up to the winds and storms and rains without fear. So do the strong-willed and strong-minded people, they rise against the odds and stand high towards their challenges."

∗∗∗

The glade with a fire burning in the middle of it suddenly disappeared, just as it had happened the last time. All I heard was the quiet rustling of the branches around the path underfoot. Everything around me looked normal, just the way any forest should look. Nevertheless, I sensed changes and, albeit being timid and barely noticeable, they somehow already felt very significant. Just like a tiny stem of new grass tries to push its way through the soil to the sun, as weak as it may be to start with we know its strength and might. Its will to live will get through anything, even through concrete.

I smiled inwardly, because I understood these changes were not in the surrounding forest, they were inside me. The seeds the Shaman sowed in my soul and mind had set their roots, and the first shoots had begun to peek through the surface, just like seemingly weak, yet secretly strong new green grass shoots…

Chapter Five
The cart of life

It seemed the Shaman was observing the changes happening to me very closely, just like a farmer watches over his harvest. Every farmer knows you should fertilise and water the fields. When Wind of the North sowed the first crops into my mind and soul, into my heart, he began nurturing them. The Shaman certainly made sure the seeds would grow into a lush harvest.

※※※

It was not even a month since our last conversation and we had met again. This time, just as I stumbled over the same tree's root bulging through the foot trail I already knew what I would be asking my trusted and wise teacher. Therefore, as soon as the recognisable yet non-familiar song began, and both our spirits left their bodies and

Chapter Five: The cart of life

placed themselves nearby, I asked the question:

"What is human life?"

This was the first time the Shaman hesitated with his reply and appeared to be thinking, rather than responding straight away as he had done every time before now. I am convinced he did know the answer though, most likely he was deliberating whether to offer me his interpretation of life or not, whether I was ready to hear his answer. With my heart doing somersaults inside my chest, I watched his face and waited.

"Imagine a horse-drawn cart moving up a hill. When you feed the horse it will pull the cart with its energy and strength, with all its force. While the horse is being nourished and cared for by its owner, it will pull the cart and continue moving up the hill. This is the cart of your life that keeps moving, being driven by your energy and your desires. Not long after you stop feeding the horse it will weaken and stop moving. The horse will stand still on the spot, but the cart will not. Remember, the cart has wheels, they are round, and they are designed to roll.

So where do they roll when the cart is halfway through its climb up the hill? You know the answer; the cart will roll back down the hill. The exhausted and malnourished horse will not be able to hold the cart in place, and the horse may be so weak it will get dragged down by the cart, loaded and heaving with your life thoughts, feelings, experiences and aspirations. These are your life forces and they weigh a lot. The longer that cart will roll back down the hill, the more strength you will need to stop it moving downwards let alone to stop it, and I am not even talking of bringing it back up."

The Shaman's voice sounded hoarse, like a creaky door where the hinges have not been oiled for a long time. It seemed he had not yet made the decision: whether to share this new wisdom with me, or to wait. However, as he had already begun to talk, he continued and I gratefully listened, absorbing his words and retaining them deep inside my mind and soul:

"Do not forget that not only will you have to put in a huge effort to stop the cart rolling down hill, but that after, you will need to double your efforts to repeat the same path, taking it back up the hill."

"What if I don't want to continue? What if I change my mind and choose a different path, a different hill, or a valley instead?" I asked the Shaman. I was rather puzzled by his words, and could not comprehend why, on earth, anyone would want to keep moving upwards through their entire life? What about moving sideways, keeping on the same level, or even standing still or going backward?"

"Your question is not unfounded," replied the Shaman, "And I will tell you why. Our world is in constant movement, it is a harmony of perpetual motion. Everything in life is in movement, even when it appears static. Life itself is a journey, not a destination. Everything moves, from the stars in the sky to a speck of dust in the air. When there is no wind and you look against the sun you will see many of those specks floating in the light, glistening like many miniature light-bulbs. It is not possible to stand still in the middle of the storm, or in the middle of moving traffic. You can stay in one place for some time, but it requires an effort too, and in the end you will be forced to continue your movement. You will only have two options then – either keep moving

Chapter Five: The cart of life

forward using your own might, or surrender to the external forces and let them pick you up and take you wherever they want to go. This means the direction of your movement can be anywhere, it will not be your own and may even be against your wishes."

I closed my eyes, and nearly jumped out of my skin when I felt a gentle brushing of the air against my face, like the soft weightless touch of a loving hand.

"Our life consists of constantly climbing up the hill and rolling down the hill. To ensure the cart of your life does not roll down and stay down, you need to keep up the momentum. You don't have to push or pull the cart when you are exhausted, or struggle when you have no strength. Even a slight movement is still a movement, the velocity is not critical. If you have set your sights high, the hill will be especially steep, and therefore harder to conquer, but it still will be a move in the direction of your choice. You cannot control the angle of the hill rise, but you can control the speed."

"What sort of heights can I possibly reach?" I asked. I felt curious, to say the least.

"Everyone's perception of height is different," replied Wind of the North. "Something that seems very low for one person, can be rather high for another person. To get to the top you need to be able to see it! You need to imagine yourself where you want to be, how you see yourself after you have reached that top. That is how you determine your heights.

Without a map, a person can get lost in the woods. Without basic navigation skills, he will not be able to find his way in the city. The horse pulling the cart of your life is also at risk of getting lost in the fog of your thoughts if you are not clear what your target destination is. The more certain you are about your ultimate goal, the easier will be your journey. Easier not in terms of simplicity, you will still have to work hard. It will be easier in terms of guiding your horse. The more vivid the picture of your ultimate goal is in your mind's eye, the clearer becomes the road there. If you sway, if you keep changing your mind, or if the image becomes fuzzy, the road will become longer through twists and turns on the way, and it may not even lead anywhere at all but to a hazy hilltop."

I nodded to acknowledge my understanding and to show my agreement with these words. The Shaman was now talking with no pause between his teachings, as if there were no boundaries between different aspects of a human life. It also seemed he wanted to speak faster, as if he was running out of time.

"You need to remember, young man, that when walking forward you must be looking forward. When moving upward you need to keep your head high. Don't look at the pebbles under your feet, look up and see where you are going, where you want to be. Don't look back – it is the past that should be left behind. If you keep looking down or sideways or backwards, how can you see the future? How can you see the road in front of you? All these distractions are designed to blind you and slow you down, to make you self-doubt, to steel your time from focusing and seeing your future. You must live in the present and leave the weight of the past behind."

"Perhaps," I said. I had my doubts. "It's not that easy to leave the baggage of the past behind you. Talking of the baggage

Chapter Five: The cart of life

– it is not even possible to have a good rest while on holiday!"

"This is because people have forgotten how to relax," said the Shaman with a big sigh. At the same time, the sound of his song exploded, becoming powerful like a giant ocean wave. There was an unrestrained power in his song, ready to fall on the Earth, while sweeping away everything that may get in the way of its course. It was at that moment that I realised my communication with the Shaman might be coming to an end.

"People in big cities need to learn again how to relax, to use the rare moments of rest and relaxation productively, to get all outstanding problems out of their minds, even if only temporarily. Worrying about something out of your control overwhelms you, but won't solve anything. Sadly, modern people, especially the residents of megalopolises, do not use these infrequent moments of repose effectively. Instead of taking an opportunity to relax and unwind, to recharge from nature, they dwell on and rehash the crumpled thoughts and worries that they cannot solve. They are trapped inside their minds, taken prisoners by their busy lifestyles and concerns. They lose the invaluable times of peacefulness and tranquility available to them, thereby breaking the main principle of a holiday, which should be a break from everyday fears, troubles and difficulties. They waste or misuse their vacation time and then come back even more wound up, restless, tired and anxious."

"Look around, look at nature!" he continued. "All animals take time to rest; even the predators bask in the sun and don't think about hunting and providing for themselves all of the time. They relax and regenerate, replenish their energy for later use. But people torture themselves by constantly thinking without switching off, ever. They think about the tasks not yet completed, the problems not yet resolved, the jobs not yet done. They scar themselves with these thoughts about their remaining challenges, thus turning their vacation into something absolutely meaningless and even harmful. If they did take time for that well deserved rest, they would have given themselves a better chance to face challenges. Everything takes time, and there is a time for everything. A 100-year-old oak takes time to grow from a little acorn. The soil nourishes the seed. Then it takes many years of growing and getting stronger, learning to resist against the bad weather, the wind, the animals who try to destroy the young oak. Only after going through this long process can a small shrub turn into a large tree that will withstand the harsh weather and the cruelty of animals trampling over it, and chewing up the little young plant. Most people forget that there cannot be a strong oak tree before an acorn. Likewise, there can be no successful result before your begin your walk towards your goal."

✳✳✳

A loud bang of the tambourine stopped an unfinished song. The fire had gone out, and it was cold. This time, I wasn't courteously helped to the footpath leading out of the woods. I shivered from the chilly evening air and began to seek my way out. This was only the beginning of my path, to my destination.

Will I see the Shaman again, during this lifetime? Will he help me out with his wisdom and advice? I don't know. Will I be able to learn to take those breaks to recharge my inner battery? I don't know. I am not even sure he would be able to answer all these questions. Everything depends on me, solely.

About the author

Anthony Bogrjantseff was born in Estonia. He studied music and sociology, and having completed his postgraduate education continues a life-long study and path of self-improvement. He has been published in Germany and the UK. He always writes in Russian. *Talking to a Shaman* is his first book translated into English.

One of his major interests is societal psychology, and he has developed insightful mind/spirit concepts. His goal is to share his innovative and unique way or presenting these life-improving ideas and techniques. This book, which is a first in the series of *Talking to a Shaman*, is a way to do this.

Anthony Bogrjantseff currently lives in London.

Milton Keynes UK
Ingram Content Group UK Ltd.
UKHW032225231124
451543UK00011B/368